J. O. Halliwell-Phillipps

Regnal Years

List of Law Terms, etc. during the Shakespearean Period

J. O. Halliwell-Phillipps

Regnal Years
List of Law Terms, etc. during the Shakespearean Period

ISBN/EAN: 9783337063511

Printed in Europe, USA, Canada, Australia, Japan

Cover: Foto ©ninafisch / pixelio.de

More available books at **www.hansebooks.com**

DURING

The Shakespearean Period.

COMPILED BY

J. O. HALLIWELL-PHILLIPPS.

BRIGHTON:

PRINTED BY J. G. BISHOP.

1883.

5

C. Commission.

Cert. Certificate.

D. or Dp. Deposition.

I. Interrogatory.

Inq. Inquisition.

Int. Interrogatory.

O. Order.

Rc. Recognizance.

Rj. Rejoinder.

Rp. Replication.

W. Writ.

6

1564.

1 Jany.
to   } 6 Eliz.
16 Nov.

---

17 Nov.
to   } 7 Eliz.
31 Dec.

Hilary Term, 24 Jany. to 12 Feby.

Easter Term, 19 April to 15 May.

Trin. Term, 2 June to 21 June.

Michs. Term, 9 Oct. to 28 Nov.

1565.

1 Jany.
to   } 7 Eliz.
16 Nov.

---

17 Nov.
to   } 8 Eliz.
31 Dec.

Hilary Term, 23 Jany. to 12 Feby.
Easter Term, 9 May to 4 June.
Trin. Term, 22 June to 11 July.
Michs. Term, 9 Oct. to 28 Nov.

1566.

| 1 Jany. to 16 Nov. | } | 8 Eliz. |

| 17 Nov. to 31 Dec. | } | 9 Eliz. |

Hilary Term, 23 Jany. to 12 Feby.

Easter Term, 1 May to 27 May.

Trin. Term, 14 June to 3 July.

Michs. Term, 9 Oct. to 28 Nov.

1567.

1 Jany.
to   } 9 Eliz.
16 Nov.

---

17 Nov.
to   } 10 Eliz.
31 Dec.

Hilary, 23 Jany. to 12 Feby.

Easter, 16 April to 12 May.

Trinity, 30 May to 18 June.

Michs., 9 Oct. to 28 Nov.

1568.

1 Jany.
to
16 Nov. } 10 Eliz.

---

17 Nov.
to
31 Dec. } 11 Eliz.

Hilary, 23 Jany. to 12 Feby.

Easter, 5 May to 31 May.

Trinity, 18 June to 7 July.

Michs., 9 Oct. to 29 Nov.

1569.

| 1 Jany. to 16 Nov. | } | 11 Eliz. |

| 17 Nov. to 31 Dec. | } | 12 Eliz. |

Hilary, 24 Jany. to 12 Feby.

Easter, 27 April to 23 May.

Trinity, 10 June to 29 June.

Michs., 10 Oct. to 28 Nov.

1570.

| 1 Jany. to 16 Nov. | } | 12 Eliz. |

| 17 Nov. to 31 Dec. | } | 13 Eliz. |

Hilary, 23 Jany. to 13 Feby.

Easter, 12 April to 8 May.

Trinity, 26 May to 14 June.

Michs., 9 Oct. to 28 Nov.

1571.

1 Jany.
to   } 13 Eliz.
16 Nov.

---

17 Nov.
to   } 14 Eliz.
31 Dec.

Hilary, 23 Jany. to 12 Feby.

Easter, 2 May to 28 May.

Trinity, 15 June to 4 July.

Michs., 9 Oct. to 28 Nov.

1572.

| 1 Jany. to 16 Nov. | 14 Eliz. |

| 17 Nov. to 31 Dec. | 15 Eliz. |

Hilary, 23 Jany. to 12 Feby.

Easter, 23 April to 19 May.

Trinity, 6 June to 25 June.

Michs., 9 Oct. to 28 Nov.

1573.

1 Jany.
to } 15 Eliz.
16 Nov.

---

17 Nov.
to } 16 Eliz.
31 Dec.

Hilary Term, 23 Jany. to 12 Feby.

Easter, 8 April to 4 May.

Trinity, 22 May to 10 June.

Michs., 9 Oct. to 28 Nov.

1574.

1 Jany.
to   } 16 Eliz.
16 Nov.

---

17 Nov.
to   } 17 Eliz.
31 Dec.

Hil. Term, 23 Jan. to 12 Feby.

Easter, 28 April to 24 May.

Trinity, 11 June to 30 June.

Michs., 9 Oct. to 29 Nov.

1575.

1 Jany.
to   } 17 Eliz.
16 Nov.

---

17 Nov.
to   } 18 Eliz.
31 Dec.

Hilary, 24 Jan. to 12 Feby.

Easter, 20 April to 16 May.

Trinity, 3 June to 22 June.

Michs., 10 Oct. to 28 Nov.

1576.

1 Jany.
to   } 18 Eliz.
16 Nov.

---

17 Nov.
to   } 19 Eliz.
31 Dec.

Hilary, 23 Jany. to 13 Feby.

Easter, 9 May to 4 June.

Trinity, 22 June to 11 July.

Michs., 9 Oct. to 28 Nov.

1577.

1 Jany.
to   } 19 Eliz.
16 Nov.

---

17 Nov.
to   } 20 Eliz.
31 Dec.

Hilary, 23 Jany. to 12 Feby.

Easter, 24 April to 20 May.

Trinity, 7 June to 26 June.

Michs., 9 Oct. to 28 Nov.

1578.

1 Jany.
to   } 20 Eliz.
16 Nov.

---

17 Nov.
to   } 21 Eliz.
31 Dec.

Hilary, 23 Jany. to 12 Feby.

Easter, 16 April to 12 May.

Trinity, 30 May to 18 June.

Michs., 9 Oct. to 28 Nov.

1579.

| 1 Jany.
to
16 Nov. | 21 Eliz. |

| 17 Nov.
to
31 Dec. | 22 Eliz. |

Hilary, 23 Jany. to 12 Feby.

Easter, 6 May to 1 June.

Trinity, 19 June to 8 July.

Michs., 9 Oct. to 28 Nov.

1580.

1 Jany.

  to } 22 Eliz.

16 Nov.

---

17 Nov.

  to } 23 Eliz.

31 Dec.

Hilary, 23 Jany. to 12 Feby.

Easter, 20 April to 16 May.

Trinity, 3 June to 22 June.

Michs., 10 Oct. to 28 Nov.

1581.

1 Jany.
to
16 Nov.
⎫
⎬
⎭
23 Eliz.

———————————————

17 Nov.
to
31 Dec.
⎫
⎬
⎭
24 Eliz.

———————————————

Hilary, 23 Jany. to 13 Feby.

Easter, 12 April to 8 May.

Trinity, 26 May to 14 June.

Michs., 9 Oct. to 28 Nov.

1582.

1 Jany. to 16 Nov.	} 24 Eliz.

---

17 Nov. to 31 Dec.	} 25 Eliz.

Hilary, 23 Jany. to 12 Feby.

Easter, 2 May to 28 May.

Trinity, 15 June to 4 July.

Michs., 9 Oct. to 28 Nov.

1583.

1 Jany.
to   } 25 Eliz.
16 Nov.

---

17 Nov.
to   } 26 Eliz.
31 Dec.

Hilary, 23 Jany. to 12 Feby.

Easter, 17 April to 13 May.

Trinity, 31 May to 19 June.

Michs., 9 Oct. to 28 Nov.

1584.

1 Jany.
to   } 26 Eliz.
16 Nov.

---

17 Nov.
to   } 27 Eliz.
31 Dec.

Hilary, 23 Jany. to 12 Feby.

Easter, 6 May to 1 June.

Trinity, 19 June to July 8.

Michs., 9 Oct. to 28 Nov.

1585.

1 Jany.
to   } 27 Eliz.
16 Nov.

17 Nov.
to   } 28 Eliz.
31 Dec.

Hilary, 23 Jany. to 12 Feby.

Easter, 28 April to 24 May.

Trinity, 11 June to 30 June.

Michs., 9 Oct. to 29 Nov.

1586.

1 Jany.
to   } 28 Eliz
16 Nov.

---

17 Nov.
to   } 29 Eliz.
31 Dec.

Hilary, 24 Jany. to 12 Feby.

Easter, 20 April to 16 May.

Trinity, 3 June to 22 June.

Michs., 10 Oct. to 28 Nov.

1587.

$$
\left.\begin{array}{c}
\text{1 Jany.} \\
\text{to} \\
\text{16 Nov.}
\end{array}\right\} \quad \text{29 Eliz.}
$$

$$
\left.\begin{array}{c}
\text{17 Nov.} \\
\text{to} \\
\text{31 Dec.}
\end{array}\right\} \quad \text{30 Eliz.}
$$

Hilary, 23 Jany. to 13 Feby.

Easter, 3 May to 29 May.

Trinity, 16 June to 5 July.

Michs., 9 Oct. to 28 Nov.

1588.

1 Jany.
to
16 Nov.
} 30 Eliz.

---

17 Nov.
to
31 Dec.
} 31 Eliz.

Hilary, 23 Jany. to 12 Feby.

Easter, 24 April to 20 May.

Trinity, 7 June to 26 June.

Michs., 9 Oct. to 28 Nov.

1589.

1 Jany.
to   } 31 Eliz.
16 Nov.

17 Nov.
to   } 32 Eliz.
31 Dec.

Hilary, 23 Jany. to 12 Feby.

Easter, 16 April to 12 May.

Trinity, 30 May to 18 June.

Michs., 9 Oct. to 28 Nov.

1590.

1 Jany.
to   } 32 Eliz.
16 Nov.

---

17 Nov.
to   } 33 Eliz.
31 Dec.

Hilary, 23 Jan. to 12 Feby.

Easter, 6 May to 1 June.

Trinity, 19 June to 8 July.

Michs., 9 Oct. to 28 Nov.

D

1591.

1 Jany.
to   } 33 Eliz.
16 Nov.

17 Nov.
to   } 34 Eliz.
31 Dec.

Hilary, 23 Jan. to 12 Feby.

Easter, 21 April to 17 May.

Trinity, 4 June to 23 June.

Michs., 9 Oct. to 29 Nov.

1592.

1 Jany.
to } 34 Eliz.
16 Nov.

17 Nov.
to } 35 Eliz.
31 Dec.

Hilary, 24 Jan. to 12 Feby.
Easter, 12 April to 8 May.
Trinity, 26 May to 14 June.
Michs., 9 Oct. to 28 Nov.

1593.

1 Jany.
to   } 35 Eliz.
16 Nov.

---

17 Nov.
to   } 36 Eliz.
31 Dec.

Hilary, 23 Jan. to 12 Feby.

Easter, 2 May to 28 May.

Trinity, 15 June to 4 July.

Michs., 9 Oct. to 28 Nov.

1594.

| 1 Jany.
to
16 Nov. | } | 36 Eliz. |

| 17 Nov.
to
31 Dec. | } | 37 Eliz. |

Hilary, 23 Jan. to 12 Feby.

Easter, 17 April to 13 May.

Trinity, 31 May to 19 June.

Michs., 9 Oct. to 28 Nov.

1595.

1 Jany. to 16 Nov. }	37 Eliz.

---

17 Nov. to 31 Dec. }	38 Eliz.

Hilary, 23 Jan. to 12 Feby.

Easter, 7 May to 2 June.

Trinity, 20 June to 9 July.

Michs., 9 Oct. to 28 Nov.

1596.

1 Jany.
to
16 Nov. } 38 Eliz.

17 Nov.
to
31 Dec. } 39 Eliz.

Hilary, 23 Jan. to 12 Feby.

Easter, 28 April to 24 May.

Trinity, 11 June to 30 June.

Michs., 9 Oct. to 29 Nov.

1597.

1 Jany.
to   } 39 Eliz.
16 Nov.

17 Nov.
to   } 40 Eliz.
31 Dec.

Hilary, 24 Jan. to 12 Feb.

Easter, 13 April to 9 May.

Trinity, 27 May to 15 June.

Michs., 10 Oct. to 28 Nov.

1598.

1 Jany. to 16 Nov.	40 Eliz.

---

17 Nov. to 31 Dec.	41 Eliz.

Hilary, 23 Jan. to 13 Feb.

Easter, 3 May to 29 May.

Trinity, 16 June to 5 July.

Michs., 9 Oct. to 28 Nov.

Hilary, 23 Jan. to 12 Feby.
Easter, 25 April to 21 May.
Trinity, 8 June to 27 June.
Michs., 9 Oct. to 28 Nov.

1600.

1 Jany.
to   } 42 Eliz.
16 Nov.

---

17 Nov.
to   } 43 Eliz.
31 Dec.

Hilary, 23 Jan. to 12 Feby.

Easter, 9 April to 5 May.

Trinity, 23 May to 11 June.

Michs., 9 Oct. to 28 Nov.

1601.

1 Jany.
to   } 43 Eliz.
16 Nov.

17 Nov.
to   } 44 Eliz.
31 Dec.

Hilary, 23 Jan. to 12 Feby.

Easter, 29 April to 25 May.

Trinity, 12 June to 1 July.

Michs., 9 Oct. to 28 Nov.

1602.

1 Jany.
to   } 44 Eliz.
16 Nov.

17 Nov.
to   } 45 Eliz.
31 Dec.

Hilary, 23 Jan. to 12 Feby.

Easter, 21 April to 17 May.

Trinity, 4 June to 23 June.

Michs., 9 Oct. to 29 Nov.

1603.

| 1 Jany. to 23 March. } | 45 Eliz. |

1 Jany.

to

23 March.

} 45 Eliz.

---

24 March

to

31 Dec.

} 1 James.

Hilary, 24 Jan. to 12 Feby.

Easter, 11 May to 6 June.

Trinity, 24 June to 13 July.

Michs., 10 Oct. to 28 Nov.

1604.

1 Jany.
to
23 March.

} 1 James.

24 March
to
31 Dec.

} 2 James.

Hilary, 23 Jan. to 13 Feby.

Easter, 25 April to 21 May.

Trinity, 8 June to 27 June.

Michs., 9 Oct. to 28 Nov.

1605

1 Jany. to 23 March.	}	2 James.

24 March to 31 Dec.	}	3 James.

Hilary, 23 Jan. to 12 Feby.

Easter, 17 April to 13 May.

Trinity, 31 May to 19 June.

Michs., 9 Oct. to 28 Nov.

1606.

1 Jany.
to } 3 James.
23 March.

---

24 March
to } 4 James.
31 Dec.

Hilary, 23 Jan. to 12 Feb.

Easter, 7 May to 2 June.

Trinity, 20 June to 9 July.

Michs., 9 Oct. to 28 Nov.

1607.

1 Jany.
to   } 4 James.
23 March.

24 March
to   } 5 James.
31 Dec.

Hilary, 23 Jany. to 12 Feb.
Easter, 22 April to 18 May.
Trinity, 5 June to 24 June.
Michs., Oct. 9 to 28 Nov.

1608.

1 Jany.
to   } 5 James.
23 March.

---

24 March
to   } 6 James.
31 Dec.

Hilary, 23 Jan. to 12 Feb.

Easter, 13 April to 9 May.

Trinity, 27 May to 15 June.

Michs., 10 Oct. to 28 Nov.

1609.

1 Jany.
to   } 6 James.
23 March.

24 March
to   } 7 James.
31 Dec.

Hilary, 23 Jan. to 13 Feb.

Easter, 3 May to 29 May.

Trinity, 16 June to 5 July.

Michs., 9 Oct. to 28 Nov.

1610.

1 Jany.
to   } 7 James.
23 March.

---

24 March
to   } 8 James.
31 Dec.

Hilary, 23 Jan. to 12 Feby.

Easter, 25 April to 21 May.

Trinity, 8 June to 27 June.

Michs., 9 Oct. to 28 Nov.

1611.

1 Jany.

to   } 8 James.

23 March.

---

24 March

to   } 9 James.

31 Dec.

Hilary, 23 Jan. to 12 Feb.

Easter, 10 April to 6 May.

Trinity, 24 May to 12 June.

Michs., 9 Oct. to 28 Nov.

1612.

1 Jany.
to } 9 James.
23 March.

24 March
to } 10 James.
31 Dec.

Hilary, 23 Jan. to 12 Feby.
Easter, 29 April to 25 May.
Trinity, 12 June to 1 July.
Michs., 9 Oct. to 28 Nov.

1613.

1 Jany.
to
23 March. } 10 James.

---

24 March
to
31 Dec. } 11 James.

Hilary, 23 Jan. to 12 Feb.

Easter, 21 April to 17 May.

Trinity, 4 June to 23 June.

Michs., 9 Oct. to 29 Nov.

1614.

1 Jany.
to   } 11 James.
23 March.

24 March
to   } 12 James.
31 Dec.

Hilary, 24 Jan. to 12 Feb.

Easter, 11 May to 6 June.

Trinity, 24 June to 13 July.

Michs., 10 Oct. to 28 Nov.

1615.

1 Jany.
  to   } 12 James.
23 March.

---

24 March
  to   ·   } 13 James.
31 Dec.

Hilary, 23 Jan. to 13 Feb.

Easter, 26 April to 22 May.

Trinity, 9 June to 28 June.

Michs., 9 Oct. to 28 Nov.

1616.

1 Jany.
to } 13 James.
23 March.

24 March
to } 14 James.
31 Dec.

Hilary, 23 Jan. to 12 Feby.

Easter, 17 April to May 13.

Trinity, 31 May to 19 June.

Michs., 9 Oct. to 28 Nov.

A NOMINAL INDEX.

Abhorson.
Adams, John, 1588.
Ague-check.
Ainsworth, John, 1582.
Alasco.
Allen, John, Richard.
Allen, Jeremy, William.
Anderson . . .
Andrews, Richard, 1586.
Arden, Joyce.   An aunt.
Armestead, Edward, 1634.
Armiger, Edward, 1635.
Armin, Robert.
Aston Cantlowe
Attewell, George, 1591.
Atwell, Hugh, 1609.
Audrey.
Augusten, William, 1597.
Axen, Robert, 1635.

Backstead, William, 1609.

Bare, George.

Barebone.

Barkstead, William, 1609.

Barnard.

Barne, William, 1594.

Barnes, George.

Bartle, Onye, 1603.

Barton-on the-Heath.

Basse, Thomas, 1611.

Bates, John.

Baxter, Richard, 1629.

Baxter, Robert, 1600.

Beeston, Christopher, 1598.

Beeston, Robert, 1609.

Beeston, William, 1639.

Belch, Sir Toby.

Belt, . . . 1594.

Benfield, Robert.

Bentley, . . . 1592.

Bernard.

Bickers, Nicolas, 1601.

Birch, George, 1625.

Bird, Theophilus, 1635.
Bird, William, 1598.
Blackfriars.
Blaney, John, 1609.
Blaxton, . . . 1601.
Boarner, Thomas, 1628.
Bond, Thomas, 1632.
Borne or Bourne, William, 1598.
Bottom, Nick.
Boult.
Bowyer, Michael, 1635.
Bristowe, James.
Browne, Edward, 1589.
Browne, Robert, 1586.
Bryan, George.
Buck, Sir George.
Buck, Paul, 1580.
Bullcalf, Peter.
Burbage, Richard.
Burton-Heath.
Cane, Andrew, 1622.
Carpenter, William, 1625.

Cartwright, William, 1594 and 1634

Cary, Gilbert, 1609

Castlee, Thomas, 1610.

Catling, Simon.

Cattarnes, . . . 1598.

Charlecote.

Chus, a Jew.

Clemham.

Clopton.

Cloten.

Clotpole

Cobweb.

Coines, Francis.

Cokely, . . . 1610.

Colbrand, Edward, 1600.

Collins, Francis.

Combe.

Comedy.

Condell, Henry.

Cook, William.

Cook, Alexander.

Cooke, alias Saunder.

Cooke, Lionel, 1588.
Cooke, Thomas, 1585.
Corin.
Court, Alexander.
Cowley, Richard.
Crosse, Samuel.
Cundall, Henry.
Curtain Theatre.
Curtis.
Darlowe, . . . 1594..
Davenant.
Davies, Hugh, 1601.
Dawes, Robert, 1610.
Day, John, 1604.
Day, Thomas, 1601.
Denigten, . . . 1594.
Disley or Distle, 1582.
Dogberry.
Doit, John.
Dombleton.
Donstall or Donston, James, 1595.
Double.
Dover.
Downton or Dowton, Thomas.

Drama.

Droeshout, Martin.

Dropheir.

Duke, John.

Dull.

Dumbleton.

Dunstan, . . . 1598.

Dutton, Edward, 1597.

Dutton, John, 1588.

Dutton, Lawrence, 1576.

Ecclestone, William.

Edmundes, John, 1606.

Elbow.

Elkins.

Evans, Henry, 1585.

Evans, Hugh.

Fang.

Feeble, Francis.

Feste.

Field, Nathaniel.

Fisher, Clement.

Fluellen.

Flute.

Ford, Frank..

Foster, Alexander, 1611.

Foundpot, Simon.

Fowler, Richard, 1624

Frogmore.

Frost, John, 1600.

Froth.

Fulwood, John.

Gabriel.

Gadshill.

Gam, David.

Garland, John, 1603.

Gebon.

Gerrold.

Gilburne, Samuel.

Giles, Nathaniel, 1601.

Gilliams.

Gillian.

Globe, the.

Goffe, Matthew and Robert.

Goodale. R. and Thomas, 1594.

Gough, Robert.

Gracechurch Street, Cross Keys.

Greene, Thomas.

Greenfield.

Gregory, Jack, 1594.

Greville, Curtis.

Grindstone, Susan.

Gue, . . . 1598.

Gunnell, Richard, 1623.

Hacket, Cicely and Marian.

Hall, John.

Hamlet, Robert, 1611.

Harrison, William, 1585.

Hart.

Harvey.

Hassard, Robert, 1594.

Hathaway.

Hayward, Thomas, 1603.

Hearne, Phillip, 1607. ·

Helle, John, 1597.

Hemminges, John.

Henley-in-Arden.

Herne.

Hewyns, Agnes.   An aunt.

Hill, John.   Also, a player, 1601.

Hobbes, Thomas, 1610.

Holland, J., 1594.

Honeyman, John, 1629.

Hour, Humphrey.

Howard, Thomas, 1600.

Hunsdon, Lord.

Hunt, Thomas, 1611.

Jeffes, Anthony and Humphrey.

Johnson, Gerard.

Johnson, William, 1588.

Jones, Jack and Richard, 1594.

Jonson, Ben.

Juby, Edward R., and William, 1598.

Keepdown, Kate.

Kemp, William.

Kendall, W., 1594.

Keyser, Robert, 1608.

Knell.

Lambert, Joan.　An aunt.

Laneham, John, 1574.

Langley, . . .

Lee, Robert, 1594.

Lipsbury Pinfold.

London.

Lowin, John.

Lucy, Sir Thomas.

Lumbert Street.

Lusty Pudding.

Marbeck, Thomas, 1594.

Martext, Sir Oliver.
Marton, Thomas, 1601.
Massey, Charles, 1599.
Middleton, John, 1597.
Miller, Edward.
Milles, Thobie, 1585.
Minikin, Matthew.
Monarcho.
Moore, Joseph, 1611.
Mopsa.
Moth.
Mouldy, Ralph.
Naps, John.
Nash.
Newton, John, 1610.
Niccolls, Robert, 1596.
Nightwork, Jane and Robin.
Oatcake, Hugh.
Old Stratford.
Ostler, William.
Ottewell, George.
Overdone.
Page, George, Thomas and William.
Pallant, R., 1594.
Paris Garden.

Parr, William, 1594.

Partlet.

Peers, Edward, 1601.

Penn, William, 1609.

Perkes, Clement.

Perkins, Richard, 1609.

Peto.

Phillips, Augustine.

Pickbone, Francis.

Pigg, John, 1594.

Pimpernel, Henry.

Pinch.

Players.

Playhouses.

Poetry.

Pollard, Thomas, 1625.

Pope, Thomas.

Potpan.

Pratt.

Pudding.

Puff.

Quickly.

Quince.

Quiney.

Ralph, a tapster,
Raynoldes, William.
Reason, Gilbert, 1610.
Revels.
Rice, John.
Robinson, John.
Robinson, Richard.
Rochester.
Rogoby.
Rossil.
Rossiter, Phillip.
Rowley, Samuel, 1599.
Rowley, Thomas, 1594.
Rowley, William, 1610.
Rugby.
Russell or Rossil.
Russell, Thomas.
Sadler, Hamlet.
Saunder alias Cooke. q. v.
Scarlet, Richard, d. 1609.
Seacoal, George and Francis.
Shadow, Simon.
Shakespeare.
Shallow.
Shank, John.
Shawe, John, 1599.

Shawe, Julius.

Shawe, Robert, 1597.

Shortcake, Alice.

Shottery.

Silence.

Silence, Ellen.

Simcocks, . . . 1603.

Simple.

Singer, Gabriel, 1597.

Singer, John, 1600.

Sinklow.

Slater, Martin, 1603.

Slender,

Sly, William, Christopher and Stephen.

Smile, Jane.

Smith, John, 1609.

Smith, William, 1596.

Smooth.

Snare.

Sneak.

Snitterfield.

Snout.

Snug.

Soundpost, James.

Southampton, Earl of.

Southwark.

Speed

Spenser, Gabriel.

Squash.

Squele, William.

Stage-plays.

Starveling.

Stockfish, Sampson.

Stratford-on-Avon.

Stringer, Agnes.   An aunt.

Sugarsop.

Surecard.

Swanston, Eyllardt, 1625.

Swinnerton, Thomas, 1609.

Syferweste, Richard, 1602.

Tarbox, John, 1611.

Tarlton, Richard.

Tawyer.

Taylor, R., 1594.

Taylor, Joseph.

Tearsheet, Doll.

Thayer, John, 1602.

Theatres.

Thump, Peter.

Tong, William, 1589.

Tooley, Nicholas, alias Wilkinson.

Tottnell, Henry, 1591.

Touchstone.

Towne, John, 1589; Thomas, 1597.

Townsend, John, 1611.

Tragedy.

Tucke, T.

Tucker, Leonard, 1600.

Turf, Peter.

Underhill, William.

Underwood, John.

Vaughan or Yohan.

Visor, William.

Wadeson, Anthony, 1590.

Walker, Sir Edward.

Wart, Thomas.

Warwickshire.

Webbe, Margaret.   An aunt.

Whatcot, Robert.

Wilkinson, Nicholas, alias Tooley.

Williams, Michael.

Wilmecote.

Wilson, John.

Wilson, Robert, d. 1600.

Wincot.

Windsor.

Woncot.
Worth, Ellis, 1617.
Yohan or Yaughan.
Yorick.

THE END.

J. G. BISHOP, Printer, "Herald" Office, Brighton.

www.ingramcontent.com/pod-product-compliance
Lightning Source LLC
Chambersburg PA
CBHW020337090426
42735CB00009B/1567